There is VICTORY with GOD

21 DAYS

of Declarations, Prayers, and Encouragement.

TABETHA PITTMAN

Copyright © 2020 Tabetha Pittman

Touch of Abundant Blessings, LLC

PO BOX 1583

Tallevast, FL 34270

Assisted by: Global Destiny Enterprise, LLC

Cover design by: Angela Mills Camper of Dezign Pro Printing & Graphics

Printed in the United States of America

First Printing, 2020

ISBN: 978-0-578-74655-5

DEDICATION

I dedicate my very first body of work to my heartbeats, PittFam5!

To my king, my husband, my best friend, my PPK, Jerome, my princess Niketa aka Ketaboo, my young king Jerome aka Kidd Pittman, and the prince Marshawn aka "Grandman." I hope I have been an amazing wife, mom, and Mink Mink. I love you guys and thank you for inspiring me to be the best I can be.

To my parents Carlton and Wanda, as well as to Ken, Grandma Lula and my grandfathers George and Thomas Lee who are resting in peace. To Grandma Lee Ester and my great-grandmother Elizabeth who all had a hand in raising me to be the intelligent, strong, victorious, steadfast, God-fearing, beautiful, and blessed woman I am.

Cathy "Mabel" and my wonderful late Aunt Alice always told me during our weekly hair parties, "Things are always going to be alright; you just have to trust in God, not man."

To my cousin Shaquantia "Pip" who always shows me unconditional love. She told me, "Diva, I'm always going to be proud of you no matter what. You are spiritual, funny, fun to be around; you bring life to parties and, oh, let's not forget, you can dance (her words not mine)."

To Reverend Dr. Ezell Patterson and Minister Willie C. Shaw for the many prayers, sermons, and nightly scriptures of encouragement. Having you two men of God on speed dial is such a blessing. No matter the day or night, you are both available to give me the Word of God, some healing, and even laughs.

I hope I've made you all proud of the work I put into this project and of me!

Love always,

Tabetha T. Pittman

ACKNOWLEDGMENT

First, I give honor to God my Father, Creator, Healer, and Friend through whom all my blessings flow. I thank Him for the calling He has spoken over my life. I give Him all the praises and honor for giving me a gift to help build up His kingdom.

My sarge, mentors, counselors, and spiritual parents, Yvette and Gerald Benton: you guys saw something in me I didn't see in myself. You imparted into me who God said I am; you pushed me out of my comfort zone, encouraged my spiritual growth, and opened my eyes to God's perfect plan. You both called me out when I was hiding because you knew I had it in me.

My rose, Momma Rose Rome Hammond, this woman of God has the patience of Job. Let me tell you; she kept me in check and in step. She got me all together when I was blocking what I could already hear God speaking but wasn't ready to accept. She never let me quit no matter how hard it got. Thank you.

Tisa Waiters, who would ride 1000 miles (in her words, even though we both live in Florida) just to sit with me, pray with me, and lift me up. She never let me down and would travel another 1000 miles to make sure I'm good and to put her eyes and hands on me.

Sabrina Bowman, who kept me encouraged and checked on me constantly. You keep me laughing and never judge me. Your soothing voice and warm spirit let me know everything will be okay.

Nicole "Cole World" Stephens, every day, you kept me in such good spirits. Your friendship has been nothing but pure love, laughter, and fun. You have a genuine heart, and you bring joy and love for everyone, even on cloudy days. No matter where we are, I will always come down to your office to bust a move.

Tabathia Daniels, who told me, "You're such a beautiful person inside and out with a good heart, so believe God for a supernatural turnaround. It's hard but keep fighting! You can't let the Devil dance because that's what he wants. You're going to stomp the Devil right out of your life." I'm stomping Sis!

LaWanda Barber, who prayed for and encouraged me to get to know God intimately in worship, praise, and spending time with Him. Thanks for encouraging me to let Him show me how much He loves me.

Ina Thomas, for the prayers, as well as for keeping me laughing, and in the right fighting spirit. You have the best comeback jokes, quick wit, and a genuine, loving heart.

Last but definitely not least, Jasma Starks, my writing coach. You didn't frown at my concept; You prayed for me and this project. You walked me through the process with kid's gloves until it was birthed. Thank you for everything.

TABLE OF CONTENTS

INTRODUCTION

"Thou shalt decree a thing, and it shall be established unto thee and the light shall shine upon thy ways" (Job 22:28, KJV).

In this book of declarations, prayers, and devotions, you'll ask yourself: why do I need to know how to decree and declare? What is the purpose of this? What will I gain from doing this?

Dictionary.com using the Oxford language defines the word "decree" as an official order issued by a legal authority. God gives us the legal authority to decree over ourselves and circumstances.

To "declare" means to affirm, protest, imply, making something known emphatically, openly, or formally. To declare is to make known, sometimes in the face of actual or potential contradiction (Dictionary.com).

So when you're reading these declarations, you are telling (declaring) Satan, "God has given me authority (decree) to kill you where you stand. He has also given me strength, power, and boldness to tell you to your face that your days of trying to destroy me, interfere with my life, harass anyone who shares my DNA, and anyone attached to me are over." You do so without messing up your hair, breaking a sweat or a nail.

As you take this 21-day journey with me, I hope you will understand why we declare and feel a sense of freedom knowing that you too have been given this legal authority. Allow God into your life to help you. You are a "peculiar" person who can assassinate Satan and all his minions from your life.

Each day, you will meditate on what you have read and write down your thoughts in the space provided. I encourage you to reflect on the declarations and prayers, incorporate them into your day, and live with a fresh, renewed vision and focus on what God has already spoken into your life.

The authority to take your life back from that demon is yours. All you have to do is accept it!

DAY ONE
GOD IS IN THE HEALING
BUSINESS

"He will wipe away every tear from their eyes and death shall be no more, neither shall there be any mourning, nor crying, no pain anymore, for the former things have passed away" (Revelation 21:4, ESV).

As we move through the healing process, to get total deliverance, our hearts must be healed, clean, and pure. You cannot expect to move forward in your God-given journey still carrying the pain of a broken heart; it simply will not work. You will continue to live in the agony of what has hurt you. However, if you surrender your life to God, He will give you the heart transplant you need to be completely delivered.

DECLARATIONS

- I take full authority over everything that has tried to keep my heart from being healed by the Holy Spirit.
- My flesh and heart may fail, but God is the strength of my heart and my portion forever (Psalm 73:26, ESV).
- My Father is near to the brokenhearted, and He saves the crushed in spirit (Psalm 34:18, ESV). He has made my heart pure and I am clean from all my sins (Proverbs 20:9, ESV).
- I love You, Father with all my heart, soul, and mind (Matthew 22:37, ESV).
- You are an awesome God. Life and favor are upon me. Thank You for healing me.

PRAYER

God, You declared that You are pulling me from the entangled roots of my past. You are protecting and holding my heart in Your hands, so no one can ever cause me any hurt, pain, or shame. You performed open-heart surgery on me; no longer do I carry those infirmities that have tried to destroy me, harden my heart, and make me think life's not worth living.

God, You have pumped pure, clean blood into me to flow from my heart. Your blood is made of Your *agape* love, grace, and mercy. Your blood makes my heart beat strong and empowers me to work hard and please You. As You heal my brokenness and bind up my wounds (Psalm 147:3 ESV), forgiveness and deliverance replace the pain. I can feel the clean, pure blood flowing through newly unclogged arteries. It delivers love, peace, joy, patience, and understanding from the top of my head down to the soles of my feet.

Your blood gives me a heart so close to You that no further harm can come to me or anyone who shares my DNA. My Father, You have created a pure heart in me and renewed a steadfast spirit within me

6

(Psalm 51:10, ESV). You said, "My child, your heart is healed and protected by My healing hands." Your love bears all things, believes all things, hopes all things, and endures all things (1 Corinthians 13:7, ESV). I thank You, Father, for the peace You leave with me. Your peace doesn't allow my heart to be troubled. It does not let me be afraid of anything (John 14:27, ESV). The peace of my Father, which surpasses all understanding, will guard my heart and my mind (Philippians 4:7, ESV). I will trust You, Lord with all my heart. I will not lean on my own understanding. Everything I do with my renewed heart, mind, and spirit will acknowledge all You have done for me, where You have brought me from as I look forward to the beautiful signs, wonders, and miracles ahead of me (Proverbs 3:5-6, ESV).

I will praise You forevermore, Amen.

What revelation was downloaded into your spirit from your devotional reading?

_____

_____

_____

_____

_____

_____

_____

_____

_____

_____

_____

_____

_____

_____

_____

_____

_____

_____

_____

DAY TWO
GOD WILL GIVE YOU CLEAN HANDS

"Beloved, never avenge yourselves, but leave it to the wrath of God, for it is written, "Vengeance is mine, I will repay, says the Lord" (Romans 12:19, ESV).

As kids, we saw adults in our lives go through mental and physical abuse at the hands of people who were supposed to love them. Consequently, we grew up thinking the abusive environment we lived in was normal. We think it's okay to be beaten, called names, and be treated badly just to feel loved. This is not so. God never said we should accept abuse as normal behavior. As His children, we have the authority to end this now! Don't let your children think this is the way to live. They will live what they learn. End this ugliness now, not with fists, bullets, or knives but with the Word of God.

DECLARATIONS

- Father who art in heaven, on this day, I dismantle all generational curses of physical and mental abuse.
- I evict the spirit of resentment and decapitate all negative thoughts of revenge and unforgiveness.
- I apply the blood of Jesus to mend the wounded hearts and end all of the crying and grief.
- God said, He will never leave me or forsake me (Joshua 1:5, ESV). The Lord will fight for me. I only need to be still (Exodus 14:14, ESV).
- If my Enemy is hungry, I will feed him; if my enemy is thirsty, I will give him something to drink; for by doing so, I will heap piles of burning coals on his head.
- From this day, I am no longer overcome by evil, but I overcome evil with good (Romans 12:20-21, ESV).

PRAYER

Eternal Father, who sits high and sees all on the earth, with a broken and wounded heart, battered body, and vengeful mind, I come to You for healing from those painful blows and disgusting words. Father, I am nothing I've been called. Though anger has arisen in my flesh to seek revenge, I will not repay evil for evil or reviling for reviling. On the contrary, I turn the other cheek, not as a coward or a chicken but to obtain Your blessings (1 Peter 3:9, ESV).

Instead of fighting back physically, I release my tormentor to You, Daddy. As Your chosen one, holy, beloved, and with a compassionate heart, I will forgive as You have forgiven me (Colossians 3:12-13, ESV).

I declare the fruit of the Spirit over my mind and heart. Fill me with love, joy, peace, longsuffering, kindness, goodness, faithfulness, gentleness, and self-control, Lord. Fill me up daily. No longer will I think of all the negative, hurtful pain of the past (Galatians 5:22, ESV).

Your works in me are of hope in a time such as these. My God, You are faithful and You will not let me be tempted beyond my ability. Rather, You will provide a way for my escape that I may be able to endure it all (1 Corinthians 10:13, ESV). Although my flesh says fight back, I will not.

I seek You for strength. I look to You for protection. I look to You for victory after each and every fight that seems to consume me and make me feel there's no end. I know You will never leave me here alone, for I praise You, great Jehovah. I want to be where You are, Lord. I want more and more of Your faith. Bless me now, Lord. I need You every hour of this battle. The only blood I want to be covered with is the precious blood of the Lamb. I'm thankful for the blood that was shed for me and the stripes that have healed me. I am Your wonderful work, Father (Psalm 139:14, NIV). I will co-labor with You and fight against whatever tries to destroy my body, mind, heart, and soul. I know this battle is no longer mine to handle. I turn it all over to You, Father. Healing is my portion and all is well with my soul, heart, and spirit.

In the name of Jesus. Amen.

What revelation was downloaded into your spirit from your devotional reading?

_____

_____

_____

_____

_____

_____

_____

_____

_____

_____

_____

_____

_____

_____

_____

_____

_____

DAY THREE
GOD HAS WON THE BATTLE

Put on the whole armor of GOD, that you may be able to stand against the schemes of the devil. For we do not wrestle against flesh and blood but against the rulers, against the authorities, against the cosmic powers over this present darkness, against the spiritual forces of evil in the heavenly places. Therefore take up the whole armor of GOD, that you may be able to withstand in the evil days and have done all to stand firm, and take the helmet of salvation, which guides your mind and thoughts, which is the battlefield of the devil. (Ephesians 6:11-13, 17, ESV)

As we overcome life-changing events and feel they are all behind us, they tend to replay repeatedly in our heads. We cannot get these thoughts out of our minds. When we sleep and when we open our eyes, they are still there. Each day, we cry and scream but don't understand why. This is exactly what Satan wants. He wants us to remain in a state of emotional distress, so we yell, scream, and cry, not knowing we don't have to remain in this place of self-pity, in the land of Lodebar (2 Samuel 9:1-13, ESV).

DECLARATIONS

- Father, God, I send forth the Holy Ghost fire to the generational curse of emotional instability and plead the blood of Jesus over the spirit of sadness.

- I shatter the feeling of rage caused by hurt.

- I take full authority over bound and blocked mindsets.

- I declare and decree that I've uprooted control over my emotions, demolishing all outbreaks and scattering all feelings of sadness.

- In Your Word, Father, You said I am quick to hear, slow to speak, and slow to anger, for the anger of man doesn't produce the righteousness of God (James 1:19-20, ESV). You are with me, Lord. I am strong and courageous. I will not be frightened or dismayed because You are with me everywhere I go (Joshua 1:9, ESV).

PRAYER

Lord, I ask You to command the rage inside my mind when I feel enmity against those who have hurt and taunted me. Deliver me from myself, Lord, from all of my overthinking and everything that causes me to hurt myself. I pull up from the root the spirit of uncontrollable emotions.

Lord, please don't let any temptations overtake me. You are faithful and will not let me be tempted beyond my ability. When temptation comes, You provide a way for me to escape, so I can endure it all (1 Corinthians 10:13, ESV). I have control over my thoughts and emotions. I can focus on reality and the mighty work You are doing in me. No longer will I let the Enemy cloud my mind with untruths. I will listen to You, God. You have known me all my life, and You have watched me constantly. You have already told me my thoughts are not Your thoughts, and my ways are not Yours (Isaiah 55:8, ESV). When You speak to me, I know what my future holds.

Satan, you have no power over me or my life. Get back to the pits of the abyss from which you love to cause so much trouble. The peace of my Father rules in my heart, and I am thankful that He loves me enough to cover me (Colossians 3:15, ESV). In the mighty name of Jesus. Amen.

What revelation was downloaded into your spirit from your devotional reading?

_____

_____

_____

_____

_____

_____

_____

_____

_____

_____

_____

_____

_____

_____

_____

_____

_____

_____

DAY FOUR
I AM A BELIEVER

"But let him in faith, with no doubting, for the one who doubts is like a wave of the sea that is driven and tossed by the wind. For that person must not suppose that he will receive anything from the Lord: he is a double-minded man, unstable in all his ways" (James 1:6-8, ESV).

During our journey to step out of the shadows of our minds, we constantly wonder if God sees us. We ask, "Do You understand what I'm dealing with? Don't You see all of these bad things that happen to me over and over again? God, don't You love me at all? Do I really have to deal with this?"

You are on your way to just giving up. You want to take it all back from God and deal with it your way. You are sick and tired of being sick and tired, not wanting to wait for the answer from God. But He's always there. All He asks us to do is be still and know that He is God (Psalm 46:10, ESV). He is God alone. He doesn't need any help from us.

DECLARATIONS

- Father, today I plead the blood of Jesus and come against all the double-minded thoughts of the Enemy.

- I firmly pull up from the root fear, doubt, and worry. I set it ablaze with Holy Ghost fire and crush all mind-blocking spirits under my feet.

- Abba, as I draw nearer to You, pull me in and cleanse my hands. Purify my heart and double-minded thoughts (James 4:8 ESV).

- I have full confidence that anything I ask You, Father, You hear me, and Your will is done (1 John 5:14, ESV).

PRAYER

Eternal and everlasting Lord, I know Your love is all I need to sustain me. Father, deliver me from myself and my overthinking. Do not allow fear, doubt, and worry to take over my life.

It is Your strength, healing, comfort, peace, joy, and all of Your promises that are with me. I believe You God for the restoration of my life, family, and finances. I believe all things will work out for my favor and good. Because You love me so much Your best is what You have for me. I just want to thank You, Lord.

I look to the hills from whence cometh my help, I know all of my help comes from You, Father (Psalm 121:1-2, ESV). God, because You love me so much You allowed my brother, Jesus, to be convicted of crimes He never committed. He took the punishment of being whipped, beaten, and dragged through the streets on His way to Calvary. He did this as payment for the crimes You knew we would commit against You. Because of His stripes and the blood He shed, I am healed (Isaiah 53:5, ESV). You didn't have to do all You did for me. I'm elated You never let go.

Thank You, Father, for giving me power when I am weak. You increase my strength when I'm exhausted, about to fall, and ready to give up on You. You grant me renewed strength, to rise up as strong as the eagle. I will run and not be weary. I shake the feeling that I am about to faint, and I walk with full might (Isaiah 40:29-31, ESV). Who can defeat me? Who can take me off my game now? No one! I have been given Your force and hardiness.

Daddy, God, You are a sun and shield. You have bestowed favor and honor upon me. You withhold no good thing from me as I walk uprightly (Psalm 84:11, ESV). I have cast down my imaginations and every high thing that exalts itself against Your knowledge, bringing into captivity every thought to Christ (2 Corinthians 10:5, ESV). Whatever I ask of You, Father, I will receive. I am an obedient child, and I keep Your commandments.

There's nothing I can ask for that You won't provide for me. I do all things that are pleasing in Your sight (1 John 3:22, ESV). God, I submit my whole self to You. I resist the Devil and all of his minions; they have no choice but to flee from me (James 4:7, ESV).

I am walking in Your love; there is nothing to fear, nothing to worry about, and not one doubt can cloud my judgment. Your Word has shown me that if I am sober and vigilant, I have a clear mind to see when the Adversary approaches me like a roaring lion, trying to pull me down (1 Peter 5:8, ESV). He will never win. I have the might of an army of 10,000 angels behind me; when he sees them, he will coward away like a kitten.

I do not know the complete plans You have for me, Father, but I do know that it is not for evil, heartache, or pain. You do not wish Your children to feel hurt or have pain; what You have for my future is bright as a diamond and has promise, as well as purpose (Jeremiah 29:11, ESV). Trouble doesn't last always but when it comes, I will call on You, Father, to take it away.

In Jesus' mighty name. Amen.

What revelation was downloaded into your spirit from your devotional reading?

_____

_____

_____

_____

_____

_____

_____

_____

_____

_____

_____

_____

_____

_____

_____

_____

_____

_____

DAY FIVE
I AM OBEDIENT

"For I know how rebellious and stubborn you are. Behold, even today while I am yet alive with you, you have been rebellious against the Lord. How much more after my death" (Deuteronomy 31:27, ESV)!

We normally put our feet down and turn away from God when nothing is going right in our lives. We don't know why hard times continue to happen, so we develop a hatred for God. No one can tell us anything about Him, say anything godly, or even encourage us to pray. It's the seed Satan planted because of all the hell we are facing. So instead of listening to the Holy Spirit, we rebel, harden our hearts, develop "I don't care anymore" spirits, and let Satan use us, especially since we already think God is against us. Not today, Satan! Our minds are free of your tricks. We refuse to be hard-headed!

DECLARATIONS

- Father, I declare and decree that I force out the spirit of stubbornness and rebellion hindering my growth.
- I pull up by the root that stiff neck that prevents me from being taught or led by the Spirit.
- Lord, I am willing and obedient to You, and I shall eat the good of the land.
- I refuse to rebel; therefore, I will not be eaten by the sword as you have spoken (Isaiah 1:20, ESV).
- I will listen to You, Lord. Deliver me from the stubbornness of my heart as I am far from righteousness (Isaiah 46:12, ESV). Please be with me always, Father (Matthew 28:20, ESV).

PRAYER

Lord, I can do nothing on my own; as I hear, I judge, and my judgment is just because I seek not my own will but Yours (John 5:30, ESV).

I am sober-minded and watchful because my adversary, the Devil prowls around like a roaring lion, seeking someone to devour (1 Peter 5:8, ESV). I have ears to listen to the directions given by the Holy Spirit.

My heart is clean and pure to accept Your requests, Lord. My eyes are open and no longer cloudy by my selfish desires to always be right. My mouth is guarded to know what to say, when to speak, and to allow the Spirit to lead and guide me.

I am disciplined and have Your knowledge. I shall obey You and Your will; this pleases You (Colossians 3:20, ESV). I will keep and follow Your commandments (John 14:15, ESV).

God, You have given me the power, love, and self-control to accept being corrected when wrong and to be led in the path of righteousness (2 Timothy

1:7, ESV). Almighty, cleanse me from all the guilt of my sin and rebellion against You (Jeremiah 33:8, ESV).

Flexibility, obedience, submission, and discernment are my portion. I will pay attention to Your voice and obey it (Exodus 23:21, ESV). I am forever at Your feet seeking forgiveness and the healing of a hardened heart. I humble myself under Your mighty hand so that You can use me. I am teachable. I am obedient to Your Word. I am no longer rebellious, stubborn, or unteachable. As Your blessed child, I will continue to hear Your words and will keep them (Luke 11:28, ESV). God, I give You all the glory and honor. Amen.

What revelation was downloaded into your spirit from your devotional reading?

_____

_____

_____

_____

_____

_____

_____

_____

_____

_____

_____

_____

_____

_____

_____

_____

_____

_____

DAY SIX
DEATH TO THE FLESH

"For jealousy makes a man furious and he will not be spared when he takes revenge" (Proverbs 6:34, ESV).

That's mine; that's mine, and that's mine, too. Anything given to us as a gift, what we have worked for, or even someone we love, we hold on to as tightly as we can because we are afraid of losing it. If anything or anyone tries to take what is ours, we become possessive and the old green-eyed monsters jealousy, selfishness, and envy lash out to keep hold. Having such a strong grip on these possessions can cause you to lose them.

DECLARATIONS

- I take full authority over the spirit of jealousy and possessiveness, for where jealousy and selfish ambition exist, there will be disorder and every vile practice (James 3:16, ESV).

- When I was still of the flesh, for a while, there was jealousy and strife. I behaved according to my human nature (1 Corinthians 3:3, ESV), and there was no way of changing my mind or my behavior. But God has done a new thing in me. These chains have been broken off of me. I have been crucified with Christ.

- It is no longer me who lives but Christ who lives in me.

- The new life I live now is not of my flesh but in the faith of my brother, Jesus. He loves me so much He gave Himself for me (Galatians 2:20, ESV).

PRAYER

Lord, You said no temptation will come to me except what is common to mankind. For the works of the flesh are evident: sexual immorality, impurity, sensuality, idolatry, sorcery, enmity, strife, jealousy, fits of anger, rivalries, dissensions, divisions, envy, drunkenness, and orgies. Those who partake in these things will not inherit Your kingdom (Galatians 5:9-11, ESV).

I cancel the jealousy in my heart and mind, for it has caused such fear, weariness, and doubt that happiness could never be in my life.

I accept the actions of love, kindness, and trust that are before me. I will no longer be consumed by my thoughts of failure and having a loser spirit. I will not worship any other god, for You, Father, are a jealous God (Exodus 34:14, ESV).

Father, I know You walk with me beside the still waters and restore my soul. You anoint my head with oil and Your rod and staff comfort me (Psalm 23:2, 4-5, ESV). I submit my whole self to You, Father. I resist the Devil, and he will flee from me (James 4:7, ESV). Abba, You will bring forth the truth to my eyes, and it will surely set me free (John 8:32, ESV).

Eternal Father, I will not forget what You have taught me. My heart will keep Your commandments all the days of my life. Peace is upon me daily. I am steadfast in love and faithfulness; I wear them around my neck and will write them on my heart. I find favor and good success in Your presence, Lord. I trust in You with all my heart, and I have my eyes focused on You. I lift up my eyes to the hills, from where all of my help comes. All of my help comes from You, Lord (Psalm 121:1, ESV). Amen.

What revelation was downloaded into your spirit from your devotional reading?

_____

_____

_____

_____

_____

_____

_____

_____

_____

_____

_____

_____

_____

_____

_____

_____

_____

_____

_____

DAY SEVEN
THERE IS PEACE IN GOD

And the Lord's servant must not be quarrelsome but kind to everyone, able to teach, patiently enduring evil, correcting his opponents with gentleness. God may perhaps grant them repentance leading to a knowledge of the truth, and they may come to their senses and escape from the snare of the devil, after being captured by him to do his will. (2 Timothy 2:25-26, ESV)

When you first wake up to start a new day, you always say to yourself, "Thank You, God, for a new day. Today, I will not let anything or anyone bother me, get on my nerves, or make me behave ugly." There's always that one person, one thing, one situation that will push you over the edge. That one annoyance will make you the pettiest of the petty. You call that person everything but a child of God.

But God says, "Today is not the day to get out of character or forget the new work I am doing in you. Today, you are representing Me. Hold your peace and go about doing My business."

DECLARATIONS

- In the name of Jesus, I force out the spirit of offense and dismantle the feeling of mistreatment.

- I will not get angry or sin. I will not let the sun go down on my anger (Ephesians 4:36, ESV).

- I appeal to You, Lord, and will watch out for those who cause divisions and create obstacles by living contrary to the doctrine You have taught. I shall avoid them at all times. These types of people do not serve You, Father. They serve their own appetites by smooth talking and flattery. They can deceive the hearts of those who listen and believe them, even if what they are saying makes no sense (Romans 16:17-18, ESV).

- The spirit of exploitation and memory recall is consumed by fire and the remnants are stomped out under the heel of my boot.

- I have good sense and am slow to anger.

- By Your glory, I overlook the offense that is against me (Proverbs 19:11, ESV).

PRAYER

Father, in the name of Jesus, Your precious peace and discernment are my portion. No one or anything shall bother or annoy me today. Your patience and strong will shall carry me through whatever or whoever is affecting my joy, happiness, or peace. I do not take to heart all the things people say. I know if my heart curses others and immediately, it is your forgiveness I ask for (Ecclesiastes 7:21-22, ESV).

I do not take vengeance or bear a grudge against anyone. I shall love my neighbor as myself because You are my Lord, Father, and Savior (Leviticus 19:18, ESV). I will be quick to hear, slow to speak, and slow to anger (James 1:9, ESV). You have given me two ears and one mouth for a reason. Two ears to listen closer to Your voice when these spirits try to flood my mind and one mouth to pray, speak with sweet words, and keep it zipped. Father, You have given me the tongue of the learned that I should know how to speak a word in season to those who are weary. You awaken me every morning; You wake up my ears to hear (Isaiah 50:4, ESV). You give me peace and patience to walk through the day without letting everything take control over my emotions or life. You are greater than anything the Enemy comes against me with.

My joy and happiness are more important than letting Satan take me out of my element. I will not wallow in the dirt with him or let him stop me from seeking Your kingdom. I am unbothered by any shade Satan tries to throw my way. My eyes and mind are covered by Your love, Father. My feet are covered in the gospel of peace. Every step I take is of joy and self-control. In the merciful name of Jesus. Amen.

What revelation was downloaded into your spirit from your devotional reading?

_____

_____

_____

_____

_____

_____

_____

_____

_____

_____

_____

_____

_____

_____

_____

_____

_____

_____

_____

DAY EIGHT
LET IT GO AND LET GOD

"And the Lord's servant must not be quarrelsome but kind to everyone, able to teach, patiently enduring evil" (2 Timothy 2:24, ESV).

When someone does us wrong or comes at us with negativity and anger, as humans, we want to strike back with vengeance and cut them to the core to get the last word. Thus, we say things we really don't mean, words used out of anger and hurt. Before you say another word, stop and think; what is this really doing? Who is truly winning? What trophy, plaque, or ribbon did you get for your trophy case? None. All you got was more heartache, hurt feelings, and the Devil pointing and laughing at the entire situation. Satan is the only one who wins during arguments, fighting, separation, and ruckus. Today, we're going to shut up, let go, and let God.

DECLARATIONS

- Lord, I dismantle the spirit of strife and combat the arguing spirit. A soft answer turns away wrath but a harsh word stirs up anger (Proverbs 15:1, ESV).

- My Father will fight for me; all I have to do is be silent (Exodus 14:14, ESV).

- God told me not to be rash with my mouth or let my heart be hasty to utter a word before Him because He is in heaven and I am on the earth. Therefore, knowing He is watching me, my words will be few; only a fool will say words that make sense to no one but himself (Ecclesiastes 5:2-3, ESV).

PRAYER

Father, I know that every fight/battle is not mine to participate in. You said in Your Word that hatred stirs up strife, but Your love covers *all* offenses (Proverbs 10:12, ESV). No matter how hard it is or gets, walking away is easier than staying for the last word. The Enemy loves division. He celebrates in chaos and feud in my life. This is what he strives for. Once he has caused disruption and disconnection in life, He has won the battle.

I have learned Your ways, Father, and I don't let Satan take me out of my element. I quickly command the spirit of loose tongues and declare I do not have the lips of a fool (Proverbs 18:6, ESV).

I am no longer hot-tempered and stirred up in strife. I am a child of God who is slow to anger and in quiet contention. I am living in peace with all, and all is well with my heart, mind, spirit, and mouth.

When I made the decision to walk with the Lord and not in my flesh, I learned that a fool gives full vent to the spirit, but a wise one quietly holds it back

(Proverbs 29:11, ESV). God, You said I am allowed to be angry, but I shouldn't sin while feeling that emotion. I will ponder with my heart in bed but be silent (Psalm 4:4, ESV). I have been given the wisdom of my Father from above, which is pure. I am peaceable, gentle, open to reason, full of mercy and good fruit, impartial, and sincere (James 3:17, ESV).

Father, teach me to be silent; make me understand how I have gone astray (Job 6:24, ESV). I swiftly apologize when I'm wrong and even if I'm right, nothing diffuses any hard feelings than a simple apology. My mouth will no longer be a weapon to tear down another person, no matter what the issue is. I will not show up to the fight with a tongue of bitterness. Instead, I will walk away in grace and with dignity and peace. God, You said my battles are not mine to fight; they are Yours (2 Chronicles 20:15, ESV); all I have to do is sit back and let You settle the war. I will have clean hands and everything will work out in my favor. I simply have to trust and believe in You alone. A closed mouth will get fed by the Holy Spirit. Amen.

What revelation was downloaded into your spirit from your devotional reading?

_____

_____

_____

_____

_____

_____

_____

_____

_____

_____

_____

_____

_____

_____

_____

_____

_____

_____

_____

DAY NINE
GOD REQUIRES US TO FORGIVE

For it is an enemy who taunts me, then I could bear it; it is not an adversary who deals insolently with me, then I could hide from him. But it is you, a man, my equal, my companion, my familiar friend. We used to take sweet counsel together; within God's house we walked in the throng. Let death steal over them; let them go down to Sheol alive; for evil is in their dwelling place and in their hearts, (Psalm 55:12-15, ESV)

The old saying is true; some people come into your life for seasons, and you can learn life lessons from them. Some friends can lift you up and be there for you. However, others have their own agendas. Not everyone you call "friend" was sent to be that. Some will hurt, shame, abuse your trust, and talk behind your back. I believe the O'Jays made a whole song about them called "Backstabbers." But no matter what they have done against you, how they try to bring you down or humiliate you for laughs and giggles, God says forgive them and learn from each betrayal. It was part of your growth and healing. Charge it to the game and thank them for the blessing.

DECLARATIONS

- Father God, I declare, decree, and send Holy Ghost fire to all ungodly soul ties.

- I break every bond and relationship outside Your will that let the Devil in.

- Whatever Satan has on me, I loose it from my mind, heart, soul, and body.

- I annihilate and take full authority over it. In the name of Jesus.

- I will not be deceived by bad company or friends, as they ruin good morals (1 Corinthians 15:33, ESV). Not all people have the Spirit of God; therefore, I will test them to see whether they are sincere. I am fully aware of the many false friends who have been sent out into the world (1 John 4:1, ESV).

PRAYER

My Lord, free me from all my deadly sins. Bring me back into Your fold. Heal me and build me up where I am weak. Give me Your strength, wisdom, and knowledge to do all things under You quickly and swiftly. In the name of Jesus. Please order my steps so I know Your goodness. God, I will seek You in my time of trouble, and You will direct my path.

I will not fret because of those who are evil or be envious of those who do wrong against me, those who lie to my face, hurt me, secretly plot and scheme behind my back. I send Holy Ghost fire against those who try to harm me. I sever the ties of all strongholds and soul ties that are hindering my growth and my walk with You, God. You said no weapon turned against me will succeed. I will silence every voice that rises up to accuse me. The benefits of being in Your presence allow You to vindicate me. You shall fight for me (Isaiah 54:17, NLT). My hands are clean, but my Father's are mighty.

The grass will soon wither. Like green plants, they will soon die away. I trust in You Father and do good. I will dwell in the land and enjoy safe pastures (Psalm 37:1-3, ESV).

Father, I will weep no longer. You said You will certainly be gracious to me at the sound of my cries for help. When You hear, You will answer me (Isaiah 30:19, ESV). With You in my life, I've learned what You desire of me. When my enemy is hungry, I will give him bread to eat; and if he is thirsty, I will give him cold water to drink. These kindhearted jesters will make those who have disrespected me, talked bad about me, tried to hurt me, slandered my name and tried to drag me through the mud feel heaping coals of fire upon their heads. And Lord, You shall still reward me (Proverbs 25:21-22, ESV).

Father, You have forgiven all my sins, so who am I to judge anyone who is trying to make amends. I have done as You have asked me. It is Your forgiveness and acceptance I seek forevermore. Amen.

What revelation was downloaded into your spirit from your devotional reading?

_____

_____

_____

_____

_____

_____

_____

_____

_____

_____

_____

_____

_____

_____

_____

_____

_____

_____

DAY TEN
GOD IS A PROMOTER!

"But he said to me, 'My grace is sufficient for you, for my power is made perfect in weakness.' Therefore I will boast all the more gladly of my weaknesses, so that the power of Christ may rest upon me" (2 Corinthians 12:9, ESV).

It is day ten and we are halfway through our devotions and declarations. Nothing can stop us from elevating but our minds. We must consistently keep our minds free from the Enemy. We discussed the full armor of God earlier; now is the time to make a conscious effort to put on the helmet of salvation daily. The Devil wages war against us in our minds/thoughts and make us think we can't reach our full potential. We will always be one step behind and trying to catch up. If we continue to let our thoughts hinder our growth, we will never walk in God's perfect plan for new levels of promotions and advancement in His kingdom.

DECLARATIONS

- In the name of Jesus, I take full authority over the spirit of rejection and apply the blood of Jesus over the spirits of fear and judgment.
- Fear has caused me not to step up and do what God called me to do, but I will not fear being judged or ridiculed. Father, You said in Your Word that if the world hates me, I should remember it hated You first (John 15:18, ESV).
- Mind crippling fear that hinders elevation from level to level I reject you.
- My father and mother may have forsaken me, but my Father in heaven has taken me in and showed me the greatest love of all (Psalm 27:10, ESV).

PRAYER

With the full authority given to me by my Lord, Jesus, Savior Christ, I declare and decree nothing the world says against me will turn me away from understanding where You want to take me. When You heard me cry for help, You delivered me from all of my troubles. My Father, I thank You for being near in my brokenness and saving my crushed spirit.

I carry many afflictions but You, mighty great Jehovah deliver me out of them all without a scratch or broken bone (Psalm 34:17-20, ESV). Not even condemnation can turn me from this walk. I desire Your Spirit, Father. I have the Spirit of life in Christ Jesus, who shed His blood for me and set me free from the law of sin and death (Romans 8:1-2, ESV).

I cast down the spirit of making wrong decisions and destroy the spirit of loneliness and feelings of disapproval. God, You have created and knitted me together in my mother's womb. I praise You because I am fearfully and wonderfully made (Psalm 139:14, ESV). You have called me to be a vision of Your image. You have worked wonders in me, and I know I am well. Even when I walk through the valley of the shadow of death, I fear no evil or anything this cruel world throws at me, for You are with me every step of the way (Psalm 23:4, ESV). I will cast all my fears to You, Father. I know You care for me. You will neither permit me to fail nor let any harm come my way. Your peace and joy are my covering; they are enough. I can only imagine all the miracles You have for me. No longer will I choose the wrong things to do. I will seek You for guidance and clear understanding.

In Jesus' name. Amen.

What revelation was downloaded into your spirit from your devotional reading?

_____

_____

_____

_____

_____

_____

_____

_____

_____

_____

_____

_____

_____

_____

_____

_____

_____

_____

DAY ELEVEN
THERE'S NO TURNING BACK WITH GOD

"Answer me quickly, O Lord! My spirit fails! Hide not your face from me, lest I be like those who go down to the pit. Let me hear in the morning of your steadfast love, for in you I trust. Make me know the way I should go for in you I lift up my soul" (Psalm 143:7-8, ESV).

You have completed your first ten days of devotions. You have declared, decreed, and reflected on the Word of God. You believe the changes in your daily walk are here. But out of the blue, Satan and his homies are back to pull you down into a spirit of depression. This is the type of game he likes to play when we decide to walk with God, accept His calling, and move toward His marvelous light. Too bad Satan didn't come with a better plan because you are stronger than he is. He will not kill, steal, or destroy your life.

DECLARATIONS

- I cast the Holy Ghost fire on the spirit of depression and defeat right now. In the name of Jesus.

- I receive full healing upon my heart, mind, and soul. My Lord said the weapons will form, but He has given me the tools to make sure they don't prosper (Isaiah 54:17, ESV).

- I will have no fear because my Father is with me. God will strengthen and help me. His righteous right hand holds me up above anything the Devil tries to come at me with (Isaiah 41:10, ESV).

- I cast all of my anxieties on God because I know He cares for me (1 Peter 5:7, ESV).

PRAYER

My Father, my Savior, I come to You as Your wounded child. The Adversary has tried to break my spirit. My spirit is weak, and I do not know what to pray for at this time, but You will intercede for me with groanings too deep for words (Romans 8:26, ESV). Lord, You said in Your Word I have no fear. Instead, I have power, love, and a sound mind, which you have given me (2 Timothy 1:7, ESV). I don't and won't worry about anything. I will pray about everything.

God, I tell you what I need, and I am forever thankful to You for all You have done (Philippians 4:6-7, NLT). No matter what I see or hear or whatever the actions of others who try to bring me pain, hurt, and shame, I know I am altogether beautiful in every way.

I am strong and courageous. I am never afraid. I will never be discouraged for You, Father, are with me at all times.

Whenever I feel unloved, unimportant, or insecure, I remember that I am the daughter of the

Most High God (Ephesians 2:19, ESV). You are my Comforter, friend, and Father, the one I look to for encouragement.

Father, when You see me, You see Your child. You give me the peace, joy, happiness, and that *agape* love I seek. You are God and God alone. I look to You to fight against all my enemies. I cast the Devil and all of his nymphs back to the pits of hell from whence they came. He seeks to steal, kill, and destroy all the work You've started in me by taking this journey. He will *not* prevail because You have come so I will have life and have it more abundantly (John 10:10, ESV). At no time will you allow the Devil to devour me.

I am Your child. You have given me the tenacity and backbone to stand up against anything. I am meek and never weak, for You order my steps. You are with me daily. Because You love me, I can walk with my head up high and breathe a sigh of release. I know my Father sees me differently from what the world says I am. You rain rays of Your glory upon me.

In Jesus' name. Amen.

What revelation was downloaded into your spirit from your devotional reading?

_____

_____

_____

_____

_____

_____

_____

_____

_____

_____

_____

_____

_____

_____

_____

_____

_____

_____

_____

DAY TWELVE
GOD'S BEAUTIFUL CHILD

"I praise you, for I am fearfully and wonderfully made. Wonderful are your works; my soul knows it very well" (Psalm 139:14, ESV).

Plenty of times in our lives we sit back and wonder why not me God? Am I not pretty enough? Am I too fat? Am I not good enough? What is it about me, Lord? We retreat into our thoughts, and this leads us to depression and negative self-thoughts. This happens because we don't know what God has already said about us and how He sees us. Satan has us focused on self-destruction and hatred of how we look and feel. We let others tell us how to think, dress, and act. We manipulate our bodies and faces to fit in just to get approval and likes from people who don't even know us. This is not us, but we do it anyway because our eyes are blinded by self-hate. We refuse to see the wonderful person God made in His image.

DECLARATIONS

- When we step out of the shadows and our loathing, we can declare and decree, from this day, I evict and uproot all spirits of low self-esteem and reject generational curses of inferiority.

- Father, You said in Your Word that all who labor and are heavy laden can come to You and You will give them rest. I will take Your yoke and learn from You, for You are gentle and lowly in heart, and I find rest (Matthew 11:28-29, ESV).

- I rejoice in my suffering knowing that suffering produces endurance (Romans 5:3, ESV).

- Father, Your Word says Your grace is sufficient for me, for Your power is perfect in my weakness. I will boast all the more gladly of my weaknesses, so that the power of Christ may rest upon me (2 Corinthians 12:9, ESV).

PRAYER

Almighty God, I seek comfort in Your arms. You cradle me on Your bosom and see me as altogether beautiful; there are no flaws in me (Solomon 4:7, ESV). You spoke to me and said, "Child, do not look at your appearance or height because that is not My concern. I do not see you as people do. They look at the outer appearance, but I look at Your heart (1 Samuel 16:7, ESV). I know your heart is pure and has been healed. I sent angels to complete a full transformation of your heart and spirit. No ill-will, hatred, hurt, pain, shame, or embarrassment was seen, just pure love. You are a daughter who loves unconditionally as I do. I remove the multiple layers of blinding scales from your eyes, so that you can see the Holy Spirit with your renewed 20/20 vision."

You said, "Don't listen to the world. See the kind of love I give." I have always sought You, Father. I couldn't see because I was of the world and I didn't know You (1 John 3:1, ESV). I have accepted that I am a chosen one, royal and obedient. I can boldly proclaim Your excellence that dwells inside me. You have called me out of darkness to walk beautifully with my head held high, tall with integrity, grace, and dignity. I have no fear or timidity because your marvelous light shines through and around me (1 Peter 2:9, ESV).

Even with that grace You have given me, I will never think of myself more highly than I ought to. I will do so with sober judgment according to the measure of faith You, Jehovah, have assigned to me (Romans 12:3, ESV).

Lord, this light and glow that illuminates around me will puzzle those who never accepted my walk, mocked me, and told me to give up, or were confused about my assignment. They shall praise me with their mouths. These strangers shall see the glory of my God through and in me. What others think they know about me, heard about me, and assume they have firsthand accounts of add no value to what You say (Proverbs 27:2, ESV).

Charm is deceitful and beauty is vain, but I fear You, God. I give You all the praise (Proverbs 31:30, ESV). I give You all the honor and glory. Hallelujah! Amen.

What revelation was downloaded into your spirit from your devotional reading?

_____

_____

_____

_____

_____

_____

_____

_____

_____

_____

_____

_____

_____

_____

_____

_____

_____

_____

DAY THIRTEEN
GOD IS IN CONTROL

"If we say we have fellowship with him while we walk in darkness, we lie and do not practice the truth" (1 John 1:6, ESV).

As we grow in Christ and get our strength, sometimes the smallest things people say, what we see or what they do to us can be annoying. We can take harmless actions the wrong way and easily throw all the healing we received thus far right out the door. In the words of Momma Rose, "Don't let the Devil send you to jail or hell." This is exactly what he wants. He wants us to stop focusing on our upward march. The Devil sees we have healed our minds. We have covered our heads with the helmet of salvation, so the double-minded thoughts are being blocked by the Word of God. However, he knows another trick that is still lingering. You are sensitive and still have some hurt buried deep. So today, we pull that up from the root and quench all quick-tempered embers that can reignite at the slightest word.

DECLARATIONS

- Lord, God, my Father, You are the head of my life.

- Father, I declare and decree the blood of Jesus over the spirit of sensitivity.

- I pull up the spirit of quick-temperance and deep hurt that drives wedges in relationships, self-love, friendships, and the inability to let things go.

- A quick-tempered man acts foolishly and a man of evil devices is hated (Proverbs 14:7, ESV). A fool gives full vent but I am wise and quickly hold it back (Proverbs 29:11, ESV).

- I watch my behavior and actions, so I do not lose what I have worked for.

- I will win a full reward (2 John 1:8, ESV).

PRAYER

My Father in heaven, You comfort me and hear my voice and cries. You wipe away all my tears, deep hurt, and pain. My Father, You pick me up and show me Your way, not my own. I declare and decree that the spirit of anger, wrath, malice, slander, and obscene talk from my mouth are put away. You have ordered my mind to be set on You, not on the things of the world (Colossians 3:8, ESV). God, You have chosen me to be Your steward. I am above approach. Because I am Your child, I shall never be arrogant, quick-tempered, a drunkard, violent, or greedy for gain. Instead, I am hospitable, a lover of good, self-controlled, upright, holy, and disciplined at all times (Titus 1:7-8, ESV).

I decree and declare that all bitterness, wrath, anger, clamor, and slander are put away from me, along with all malice. Lord, Your forgiveness shields me. Your glory is the lifter of my hands (Psalm 3:3, ESV). Lord, I keep my heart with all vigilance, for out of it flows the springs of life (Proverbs 4:23, ESV). Father, let Your light so shine through me. I have the capability to point others to Your marvelous light. Lord, I understand why You allowed me to go through so much, even though I didn't see it then. I accept that it was to sharpen my skills, restore and completely heal my heart. It was to renew my mind, so I can be a walking, talking, living testimony of how wonderful You are to me. Thank You, Abba, for bringing me out of darkness, shame, hurt, and pain. Now, I can help so many others who don't know You and are struggling to find a way to You.

Every time I said, "I can't do this; I need You," You said, "Remember whose child you are." I have been crucified with Christ. It is no longer I who live but Christ who lives in me. The life I now live in the flesh, I live by faith in the Son of God who loves me and gives Himself for me (Galatians 2:20, ESV). In the name of Jesus. Amen.

What revelation was downloaded into your spirit from your devotional reading?

_____

_____

_____

_____

_____

_____

_____

_____

_____

_____

_____

_____

_____

_____

_____

_____

_____

_____

DAY FOURTEEN
I AM WEALTHY

"A good man leaves an inheritance to his children's children, but the sinner's wealth is laid up for the righteous" (Proverbs 13:22, ESV).

Bills are coming from everywhere; the kids need food and clothes, but you are still living from paycheck to paycheck with no end in sight. Whenever your back is against the wall, and you wonder when it will ever end, look to God. God said you have not because you have not asked for what you need. Being rich is okay. But having wealth so you can leave a legacy for your bloodline is great. This wealth comes from sowing seeds into good ground and seeking God for guidance. Not all blessings of wealth are of monetary value. Some come in the form of health, love, peace, happiness, and life.

DECLARATIONS

- I reject the spirit of poverty and release the spirit of wealth upon my family.
- I cancel and set ablaze the spirit of generational poverty and lack.
- I shall not be anxious about anything. But in everything by prayer and supplication with thanksgiving, I will let You know my requests.
- Your peace that surpasses all understanding will guard my heart and my mind in Christ Jesus (Philippians 4:6-7, ESV).

The Egyptians mistreated us and made us suffer, subjecting us to harsh labor, then we cried out to the Lord, the God of our ancestors, and the Lord heard our voice and saw our misery, toil, and oppression. So the Lord brought us out of Egypt with a mighty hand and an outstretched arm, with great terror and with signs and wonders. He brought us to this place and gave us this land, a land flowing with milk and honey (Deuteronomy 26:6-9, ESV).

PRAYER

Lord, release Your financial blessings and let them rain down upon me abundantly. Remove all past and present debt. All credit cards, car payments, and mortgages are paid in full. In the name of Jesus. Lord, let our bank accounts overflow with excessive funds, so we can give loans instead of needing them. Bless us above and beyond anything we could ever ask or think. I ask right now. In the name of Jesus.

My Father, I listen and know You have chosen the poor in the eyes of the world to be rich in faith and inherit the kingdom. You have promised that those who love You shall inherit everything our ancestors left behind (James 2:5, ESV). Therefore, I accept all the wealth left on the table by all who came before me. I claim and receive it a thousand times.

Mighty Abba, I am the meek and I shall inherit the earth. I shall delight in the abundance of sweet peace (Psalm 37:11, ESV).

Almighty Father, I bring all my tithes into the storehouse that there may be food in my house. You said if I open for You and follow Your voice, the windows of heaven will pour out such a blessing for me there will not be enough room to receive it (Malachi 3:10, ESV). Lord, You said I will live off the overflow. I shall leave a legacy of wealth for my children's children (Proverbs 13:22, ESV). You promised a thousand times more of each tithe, offering, and seed that has been sown. I am blessed (Deuteronomy 1:11, ESV).

You said there's nothing lacking in me. I am a doer of Your Word. I hear You say to me, "Well done, thy good and faithful servant; you have been faithful over a few things, I will make you ruler over many things. Enter into the joy of your Father" (Matthew 25:23, ESV).

I give You all the glory, praise, and honor for my blessings, healing, deliverance, and strength. I shall have exceeding and abundant wealth. You favor me because You love me more than ever.

I surrender all my finances to You. I step back and watch You work it all out in my favor. The inheritance is mine. In the name of the Most High, Jesus. Amen.

What revelation was downloaded into your spirit from your devotional reading?

_____

_____

_____

_____

_____

_____

_____

_____

_____

_____

_____

_____

_____

_____

_____

_____

_____

_____

_____

DAY FIFTEEN
FAILURE IS NOT AN OPTION

"My flesh and my heart may fail, but GOD is the strength of my heart and my portion forever" (Psalm 73:26, ESV).

As kids, we try to make sure we are the best at everything. We make straight As and do everything correctly because we don't want to disappoint our parents or others we look up to. When we become adults, we still have this same spirit. We don't want our families, friends, or God to think we have failed them. When we are broken, we try our best to fix things without seeking God for His help, so we fail over and over again. We just can't get it right. But with God, all things are not as we see them.

DECLARATIONS

- My Lord, with great boldness and force, I annihilate the spirit of failure. I know that through You all things I put my mind on can be done.

- Nothing is broken, lacking, or missing from me (Isaiah 26:3-4, ESV).

- I can do all things through Christ who strengthens me (Philippians 4:13, ESV).

- I declare and decree that the spirit of self-rejection is thwarted and demolished.

- I cast all my burdens upon You, Lord. You sustain me and never permit the righteous to be moved (Psalm 55:22, ESV).

- God is in the midst. I shall not be moved. He helps me when the morning comes (Psalm 46:5, ESV).

PRAYER

My Father, thank You for giving me the power and anointing to do anything I set my mind to do. Nothing in me has a loser spirit. You said Your steadfast love will never cease and Your mercies will never come to an end (Lamentations 3:22, ESV).

If I fall down, I don't dwell in sadness, defeat, or gloom, I return to my feet and start all over again until the task is completed. My hands and mind work together to finish all the work at hand.

You will make a new creation in me. The old has passed away and behold, the new me is present (Proverbs 26:2 ESV). Father, You didn't create any mess. I am Your obedient child.

I continue to work out my salvation with fear and trembling (Philippians 2:2 ESV). Father, You have spoken to me very clearly that I am at peace. You said in this world I will have trouble, but You have taken my heart. Therefore, I will not be overcome by this world or its standards of living (John 16:33, ESV). I didn't make it on my own; whatever happened in the past stays behind me. I strain to see what is ahead of me, and I press toward that goal for the prize of the high calling in You (Philippians 3:13-14, ESV). The treasure from the Lamb of God is priceless.

Jehovah, draw me from the pits of my own destruction and out of a miry bog. Set my feet upon a rock. Make my steps secure. You put a new song in my mouth, a song to praise to You, God. Many will see the marvelous things You are doing in my life and will wonder how I made it through it all. Some may fear, flee, and talk negatively, but they want to know for themselves how wonderful You are. With just a little touch of Your garment, they will trust in You and become living testimonies (Psalm 40:2-3, ESV). Each morning when I wake, I will not have any doubt about who I am. I am made in Your image, and I am Your precious gift. Amen.

Can you hear Him? Who did He say you are?

What revelation was downloaded into your spirit from your devotional reading?

_____

_____

_____

_____

_____

_____

_____

_____

_____

_____

_____

_____

_____

_____

_____

_____

_____

_____

_____

DAY SIXTEEN
THERE'S NO SHAME WITH GOD!

"Instead of your shame there shall be a double portion; instead of dishonor they shall rejoice in their lot; therefore in their land they shall possess a double portion they shall have everlasting joy" (Isaiah 61:7, ESV).

Life sometimes throws situations at us that we are ashamed of. Shame comes in different ways. Sometimes it comes by our actions or those of others. Harboring this shame can affect our health, our ability to look at ourselves the same, to trust others, or to come out of the hurt, shame, and embarrassment. We ask ourselves over and over again, how did this happen? What did I do? How am I going to live with this? Who can help me get this shame out of my mind or heart? God said to look to Him for our deliverance, healing, and salvation. He will put a shield about you. He is your glory and the lifter of your head (Psalm 3:3, ESV).

DECLARATIONS

- I declare and decree that I have full authority to heal the pain of shame and bitterness.
- I reject the spirit of resentment and revenge.
- I sever and decapitate the spirit of sickness that reopens old wounds.
- Father, You will help me; therefore, I am not disgraced.
- I have set my face like flint, and I know I am not put to shame (Isaiah 50:7, ESV).
- Father, in my brokenness I searched for You and You answered and delivered me from all my fears. I look to You, and my face is radiant.
- I am no longer ashamed (Psalm 34:4-5, ESV).
- Abba Father knows the days of the blameless, and my heritage will remain forever.
- I am not put to shame in evil times.
- I have an abundance of life (Psalm 37:18-19, ESV).
- God has released in me a spirit of restoration, healing, and peace, right now.

PRAYER

Father, I thank You for Your unconditional love, for seeing the inside of my heart and not my actions or the actions of others. Lord, please guide and show me Your ways. I reject deceit and hopelessness. Father, when the righteous cry for help, You hear and deliver them out of all their troubles. All who are brokenhearted and crushed in spirit are saved by Your mighty hands. So many times, I carried my afflictions heavy on my chest. But Your righteous hands deliver me out of them all. You kept all of my bones from breaking (Psalm 34:17-20, ESV).

My God, You are forever wiping away every tear from my eyes and even when I feel death is better than re-living the events over and over in my mind, and in my dreams, You said there shall be no more mourning, crying, or pain. Once we have given ourselves to You, all of those former things have passed away (Revelation 21:4, ESV). Thank You for keeping me from an early grave by removing these boulders from my life.

God, You are my rock. I'm covered by the blood of Jesus, and Your shield protects me. I cried out to

You, Father, and You answered me. You took my heart, mind, and soul, and delivered me from all my fears, doubts, and worries. I looked at You, and You said You will never be ashamed of me. I thank You for saving me from all of my troubles. You assigned Your angels to encamp around me due to my fears, and I have been delivered (Psalm 34:4-7, ESV).

I am clean from any transgressions. I am as clean as Naaman who dipped in the River Jordan seven times for healing. My flesh was restored and became clean (2 Kings 5:14, ESV). It is as clean as the morning dew and the freshly fallen snow. Nothing is impossible with You, God (Luke 1:37, ESV). Amen.

What revelation was downloaded into your spirit from your devotional reading?

_____

_____

_____

_____

_____

_____

_____

_____

_____

_____

_____

_____

_____

_____

_____

_____

_____

_____

_____

DAY SEVENTEEN
HE IS ALWAYS PRESENT

"Look to the right and see; there is none who takes notice of me; no refuge remains to me; no one cares for my soul. I cry to you, O Lord; I say, You are my refuge, my portion in the land of the living" (Psalm 142:4-5, ESV).

Often, we feel as if God has left us alone and forgotten about us. We think He doesn't love us. These feelings come from a spirit of abandonment lingering in our lives or from childhood traumas as a result of being left behind or being treated like an orphan. In such situations, sometimes we act out because we are starving for attention. We pull away from others and God to avoid being rejected or brushed off. Our hearts become hardened toward those who left us feeling lonely, even God. He has to step in and remind us that we were never alone. He has always been our Father in heaven. All we have to do is call Him. He is always available 24/7. He will never leave or forsake us (Hebrews 13:5, ESV; Deuteronomy 31:6, ESV).

DECLARATIONS

- I shred and pull up the spirit of abandonment by the root.
- I apply the blood of Jesus to the cast away and orphan spirit.
- My God is near to me as I carry a broken heart, and He saves me from the crushing spirit (Psalm 34:8, ESV).
- I declare and decree that the spirit of feeling unloved and unwanted is dissolved and shredded from my life.
- God has spoken to me in my dreams and my ears are focused on His voice. He said "My child, neither death nor life, angels, rulers, things to come, powers, or anything in creation can separate you from My love" (Romans 8:38-39, ESV).
- God's plans for my life are good, not evil, to give me a future and hope.
- I am never alone (Jeremiah 29:11, ESV).

PRAYER

Lord God, You are my shepherd, and I lack nothing. You are my gatekeeper, and I can clearly hear Your voice. When You speak to me and call out my name, I follow. I am obedient to Your ways (Psalm 23:1, John 10:4, ESV).

Abba, thank You for loving me so much. Whatever I ask of You, You supply. As the Enemy plans his attacks against me, You have already set in place the Advocate to defend me from the assault. You give me the spirit of truth, which the world can't accept because they don't know You. I know how good You've been to me.

I have been freed from the captives who have tried to enslave me. Their curses cannot penetrate Your mighty wings that cover me. I do not fear those who kill the body because they cannot kill my soul. But I fear You, Father, who can destroy both soul and body in hell (Matthew 10:28, ESV). You have covered me with Your favor. You live in me and will continue to be with me. You will not leave me as an orphan. You will come for me. When I was lost and couldn't find my way, when I was drowning in the sea of sin, You threw out a life vest that kept me afloat. I knew it was nothing but that sweet *agape* love that saved me. On that day, I realized You were with me on the inside. You kept me because You loved me so much. Now, I can love myself fully, as well as others (John 14:15-21, ESV).

You are God alone. You strengthen, help, and uphold me with Your righteous right hand (Isaiah 41:10, ESV). You give me peace, not of this world or what the world gives. So when I'm in Your presence, my heart is never troubled or afraid (John 14:27, ESV).

I am a child who is called by Your name. I know Your power and might redeem and restore me. Father, I am here to co-labor with You. I give You all my heart's desires. All that is required is that I humble myself, turn from my wicked ways, and pray. I will hear directly from You who dwell in heaven above. All of my sins will be forgiven, and my land will be healed (2 Chronicles 7:14, ESV). Even, if my father and mother forsake me, You are watching and will take me in (Psalm 27:10, ESV). I find rest, comfort, friendship, peace, and everlasting love in Your arms. I declare and decree with all You have for me I am never alone. In the precious name of Jesus. Amen!

What revelation was downloaded into your spirit from your devotional reading?

_____

_____

_____

_____

_____

_____

_____

_____

_____

_____

_____

_____

_____

_____

_____

_____

_____

_____

DAY EIGHTEEN
THERE'S GROWTH IN CHRIST

"And that they should not be like their fathers, a stubborn and rebellious generation, a generation whose heart was not steadfast, whose spirit was not faithful to GOD" (Psalm 78:8, ESV).

The title says it all! Immaturity makes it very hard to let go of the past that has caused us to commit sin and get over rejection, hurt, shame, and pain. We would rather stay in a miserable state of mind. Once we have gone through so much, we tend to think nothing matters anymore. We lash out at everyone. We don't let anything go, and we think we're always right. Never once do we stop to consider what all this childishness, complaining, and whining is actually doing for us. The time comes when we have to put on our adult drawers, stop the madness, stop thinking God doesn't listen to us and just let it go.

That time has come! Today is that day to get your mind focused on God. Get out of your feelings. Let go of the painful past that has kept you stuck in this sunken place. It is time to rise from the ashes; wipe your face; get on your hands and knees and speak to Your Daddy as you've never done before! Today is the first day of your exodus!

DECLARATIONS

- I dismantle all generational curses of arrested development.
- I shatter all hindrances and immaturity.
- I will not continue thinking and behaving like a child. Doing so is merely a tactic of the Devil to block my spiritual maturity.
- God, Your Word says if I do not listen to You, You will discipline me again sevenfold for my sins (Leviticus 26:18, ESV).
- I repent of my sins.
- I ask to be baptized in the name of the Father, Son, and Holy Ghost.
- I grow maturely in the faith.
- I have accepted God as the head of my life.
- I put away all childish things.
- I declare and decree that this is the day I fully understand, speak, and act as a mature adult in Christ (1 Corinthians 13:11, ESV).

Almighty God because You love me so much You gave Your only begotten Son. If I believe in You, I will not perish for all of my past sins but have eternal life (John 3:16, ESV).

PRAYER

My Father, God, I pray for Your strength to pull up the spirits of rebellion, stubbornness, and strong will. I am no longer stuck in emotional immaturity. I take full responsibility for my faults and behavior. I do my best to present myself to You as You approve. I do not need to be ashamed as I rightly handle the Word of Truth (2 Timothy 2:15, ESV). The wisdom I have comes from the fear of the Lord, and the Holy Spirit's insight gives me knowledge (Proverbs 9:10, ESV).

I am no longer a child tossed to and fro by the waves and carried about by every wind of doctrine. I am not deceived by human cunning or craftiness in deceitful schemes. Rather, I'm speaking the truth in love as I grow up in every way into You, God. You are the head (Ephesians 4:14-15, ESV).

As I mature and begin to know You, I rejoice in all my sufferings knowing they have produced endurance. Endurance has produced character and character hope, change, and favor in You, God (Romans 5:3-4, ESV).

Lord, I want to be disciplined and seek knowledge. Anyone who hates correction is stupid. I love You, Father, and I will keep Your commandments (John 14:15, ESV). I pray for the spirit of discernment. I continue to love You, God, with all of my heart, soul, and mind. Thank You for strength and complete restoration (Luke 10:27, ESV). Blessed be You, Lord. You are my rock. You train my hands for war and my fingers for battle (Psalm 144:1, ESV). Whom the Son sets free is free indeed (John 8:36, ESV). I pray without ceasing because nothing is too hard for You whose hand is all over my deliverance (Luke 1:37, ESV). Father, You are the same yesterday, today, and forevermore (Hebrews 13:8, ESV). Amen.

What revelation was downloaded into your spirit from your devotional reading?

_____

_____

_____

_____

_____

_____

_____

_____

_____

_____

_____

_____

_____

_____

_____

_____

_____

_____

_____

DAY NINETEEN
SEEK GOD; HE HAS ALL THE
ANSWERS

"Beloved, do not believe every spirit, but test the spirits to see whether they are from GOD for many false prophets have gone out into the world" (1 John 4:1, ESV).

While going through daily battles, we tend to speak negative words about ourselves or our situations. We also read horoscopes or tarot cards thinking this will give us affirmative answers. Curses spoken over our lives can also keep us from believing. People who do such things see our calling but want us to fail. They don't want us to achieve anything God has for us. These words could be said because of jealousy, envy, or just pure hatred. Life and death are in the power of your tongue and those who love it will eat its fruits (Proverb 18:21, ESV). Today, we take full authority of the words we say from our lips and over any negative thoughts in our minds. We refuse to believe anyone who says anything that is not of God about our character.

DECLARATIONS

- In the name of Jesus, I declare and decree that all generational curses and witchcraft are broken.

- I call forth the Holy Ghost fire upon the curses of witchcraft, white magic, black magic, voodoo, spells, hexes, and evil words spoken over my life and family.

- All ill-spoken words and anyone dabbling in the practice of the dark world will not triumph (Isaiah 54:17, ESV).

- No weapon fashioned against me shall succeed.

- I shall condemn every tongue that rises against me in judgment.

- I am a servant of the Lord and because of my inheritance from my Father all of my vindications come from Him. Nothing is impossible for my God (Luke 1:37, ESV).

PRAYER

Heavenly Father, I release and plead the blood of Jesus over generational spirits of perversion and incest. These spirits rise and linger, but I'm a generational curse breaker for my family. These familiar spirits must be evicted and annihilated from my bloodline; no one who shares my DNA shall live in the shadows of the underworld.

Father, You said on that day, You will destroy horses from among me and demolish their chariots. You will destroy the cities of the land, all witchcraft, and curses. You will tear down all strongholds. They will no longer cast spells (Micah 5:10-12, ESV).

The fearful, unbelieving, abominable, murderers, whoremongers, sorcerers and all liars shall have their part in the lake of fire (Revelation 21:8, ESV).

When I believe and understand Your Word and power, I know repentance and prayers will make my past just. I surrender and know I belong to You because of the blood that covers me. I claim immediate victory over anyone who has spoken ill in my life and plotted destruction, as well as my downfall. These people and their practices shall never see the light of day. What they wished to cause harm over my life, You will repay them 1000 times more. You are mighty in us. You are greater than anyone or anything in the world (1 John 4:4, ESV). I decree and declare that nothing demon or evil worshippers say, cast, read, or believe in their horoscopes shall ever prosper. My God, You keep me from all harm and watch over my life. You keep watch as I come and go. You will allow nothing to hurt Your children now and forever (Psalm 121:7-8, ESV). I trust and believe that all things are possible through You, my Father who loves me.

Thank You for Your blood that was shed for me. Daddy, thank You for being my covering. Thank You for watching over me at all times. I know there's never a chance in hell that harm shall come to the godly. But the wicked shall be filled with nothing but trouble in their days ahead (Proverbs 12:21, ESV).

I implore you to seek God for forgiveness right now. In the name of Jesus. Only He can save your soul. That punishment in hell is sure to be worse than any spell you have ever cast. God is merciful. His words are truth to the believer and healing to multitudes who seek Him. He is merciful to those who repent and even the ones who refuse to. He loves all who hear and do His Word.

Today, I speak abundant life over any disparaging comments about me, my family, finances, health, and career. I am who God says I am, and I need no one else's approval. Glory to the Most High Father. Amen!

What revelation was downloaded into your spirit from your devotional reading?

_____

_____

_____

_____

_____

_____

_____

_____

_____

_____

_____

_____

_____

_____

_____

_____

_____

_____

_____

_____

DAY TWENTY
TODAY, I SURRENDER ALL TO YOU!

"If my people who are called by my name humble themselves and pray and seek my face and turn from their wicked ways, then I will hear from heaven and will forgive their sins and heal their land" (2 Chronicles 7:14, ESV).

Sin is sin no matter how you look at it, and it feels good when you're deep in it. God is reaching out to you to turn away from evil but disobedience feels so much better than walking in your purpose. You say to yourself, how can life get better than what I want to do? not knowing God wants to release generational blessings on you. But He can't because He's waiting for you to seek Him.

God has a way of getting our attention in our dreams. The nightmares try to take us out; we toss and turn. There's no sleep because the Enemy won't let us. The Enemy attacks when we're weak. He wants nothing more than to make us miserable. He calls his buddies over to help taunt us, and all we want to do is get one night of rest. At this time, we remember God is here. We cry out in pain and desperation for change, "Father, I surrender. Please forgive me." That forgiveness brings sweet sleep and peaceful rest.

DECLARATIONS

- Abba Father, I command the spirit of disobedience to no longer be my portion.
- I plead the blood of Jesus and set it ablaze on the generational curse of rebellion, right now! In the name of Jesus.
- I am a generational curse breaker. No longer will defiant behavior destroy my bloodline. Your Word teaches me through one man's disobedience many were made sinners. But through Jesus' obedience many will be made righteous (Romans 5:19, ESV).
- I know Your eyes shed streams of tears because people do not keep Your laws (Psalm 119:136, ESV) and even angels who sinned were not spared. You cast them into hell and committed them to chains of gloomy darkness to be kept until the day of judgment (2 Peter 2:4, ESV). I will honor You, Father, that my days may be long in the land You gave me.

PRAYER

Father, I come to You as humbly as I know how just to say thank You. If I had 10 thousand tongues, it would still not be enough to continually say thank You for the wonderful things You are doing in my life, where You have brought me from, and where You are taking me.

You brought me out of the pits of hell and despair. You let no harm or danger overcome me. You kept Your protective arms over me when I was at my lowest and put me back on my feet.

You wiped away all my tears. Fix my heart. Give me wisdom, strength, and peace of mind. You tell me every day that everything will be alright and work out in my favor. I just need to put my trust in You, not in man.

Father, work on me. I focus my attention on You, God. Let me hear Your voice, see what You want me to see and love how You want me to love. I will be obedient to Your Word and calling. I surrender my entire being to You as a living sacrifice. Lord, You said weapons and battles will come, but they will not prosper. You are my vindicator and protector on this battlefield called life. You surround me every day with Your angels and cover my body from the top of my head to the soles of my feet with the blood of my elder brother, Jesus. I carry Your love with me every day. I trust and believe Your Word with the faith of a mustard seed.

I trust You, Father. No matter what I see or hear, You said in Your Word You will never leave or forsake me. You don't lie. Your work in me shall come to pass. People shall see Your wonders through me, no matter what I look like on the inside. Thank You, Father, for Your grace, mercy, and unconditional love. I pray to You with an open heart and mind. Glory, hallelujah! Father, You are so worthy to be praised. I give You all the honor, God!

In the name of Jesus. Amen.

What revelation was downloaded into your spirit from your devotional reading?

_____

_____

_____

_____

_____

_____

_____

_____

_____

_____

_____

_____

_____

_____

_____

_____

_____

_____

_____

DAY TWENTY-ONE
NO BACKLASH OR RETALIATION

"Then Peter came up and said to him. "Lord, how often will my brother sin against me, and I forgive him? As many as seven times? Jesus said to him, "I do not say to you seven times, but seventy times seven" (Matthew 18:21-22, ESV).

You have come to the final day. So much has been declared, decreed, and canceled from your life. This is the day all that was troubling you, bringing you down, making you feel less than, and giving you suicidal thoughts are no longer in your spirit. Your journey is complete, but the fight is not over. The Devil is cunning and slick, so he will continue to test and tempt you, but you have the power and tools to prevent Him from taking you down.

Your final step is forgiveness of yourself and anyone who has caused you any harm. Forgiveness is not for them; it's for you. Even those who hurt you the most, God says you must forgive. When you forgive, you have done the perfect will of God.

DECLARATIONS

- My Lord, I come to You for deliverance and forgiveness for the spirit of backlash and retaliation; these demons are consumed by the Holy Ghost fire.

- Father, You said I must love my enemies and pray for those who persecute me (Matthew 5:44, ESV). I am blessed because I'm merciful.

- I shall receive God's mercy (Matthew 5:7, ESV).

- Even if I suffer for righteousness' sake, I am blessed.

- There's no fear in me.

- I am not troubled (1 Peter 2:20, ESV), for my heart, mind, and hands are clean.

- I am at peace.

PRAYER

Almighty God, on this day I ask for Your forgiveness for any actions, deeds, and thoughts that were not pleasing in Your sight. God, You said I must never take revenge but leave room for the wrath of God. You said vengeance is Yours, You will repay (Romans 12:19, ESV).

Your hand is mightier than any pettiness or revenge I can ever think of taking. You shall do to them as they have done unto me (Proverbs 24:29, ESV). Before I react and take things into my own hands, You remind me that love is patient; love is kind and is not jealous; love does not brag and is not arrogant. It does not act unbecoming. It doesn't seek its own. It is not provoked and does not take into account any wrongs (1 Corinthians 13:4-5, ESV).

Father, no matter what, I shall live like You. You have commanded me to be fervent in love for others because love covers a multitude of sins (1 Peter 4:8, ESV). I am not better than anyone who has come against me, Lord because all of us have sinned and fallen short of Your glory (Romans 3:23, ESV).

Jehovah, please forgive my trespasses as I forgive those who have trespassed against me. Father, do not lead me into temptation but deliver me from all evil (Matthew 6:11-13, ESV). I seek Your kingdom, blessings, and praises. Father, I give You all the glory and honor. Let the words of my mouth and the meditation of my heart be acceptable in Your sight, O Lord, my rock and my Redeemer (Psalm 19:14, ESV). Amen.

What revelation was downloaded into your spirit from your devotional reading?

_____

_____

_____

_____

_____

_____

_____

_____

_____

_____

_____

_____

_____

_____

_____

_____

_____

_____

_____

CLOSING PRAYER
A NEW DAY OF J.O.Y.

(Jesus Over Yourself)

"The Lord said to Moses and Aaron in the land of Egypt, "This month shall be for you the beginning of months. It shall be the first month of the year for you (Exodus 12:1-2 ESV). If you do this, GOD will direct you, you will be able to endure, and all these people also go to their place in peace" (Exodus 18:23, ESV).

Our 21-day journey is completed, but it surely isn't over. You've declared, decreed, prayed, and even written some revelations. At the end of the journey, you have accepted the assignment of our Father to surrender all to Him and say yes. Your chains of mind-blocking captivity have been shattered. You have kicked out all who were renting space in your life and not paying any bills.

What now? What are you going to do now?

Every day, you will face new challenges. Satan will try to attack you every day: blatantly or subtly. Since you've served him that eviction notice, he will try his hardest to move back in. Beware! When he comes, he will bring more freeloaders. These bums will be seven times stronger, and they will try to reclaim their spots. What will you do with your new authority?

PRAYER

Father, I have committed myself to 21 days of decreeing, declaring, and devotion. I have learned and understood that Satan will not rest until he has me back in his clutches and to my old, sinful ways. But I am ready to continue this walk. You have provided me with Your full armor. I will not allow the Enemy to overtake my spiritual growth with his own personal agendas. The spirit of offense has been canceled from my life. In the name of Jesus.

I know that every battle does not need to be won by me; therefore, I remove me out of the way. Your Holy Spirit dwells in me. Now that my journey is completed, I have learned that Satan will never stop spitting madness at me.

Your authority has released the power in me to just walk right up to him and punch him in the face with Your shield of faith. When he is down and covering his face because of that mighty blow, You have given me the strength to completely slice his head off with Your sword of the Spirit. Then, I can kick it around like a soccer ball using my feet, which are covered with Your sandals of peace.

I am not fooled. He will not cease with his attacks; there will be more. Even if he thinks he has gotten the best of me, He hasn't. I am quicker now at seeing him for what he is attempting to do. I am better equipped with weapons to help take him out. Daily, I am adjusting my helmet of salvation. I wipe off my breastplate of righteousness and tighten my belt of the gospel of truth. I stay ready for the next battle.

After completing this journey, I know You, my Father, God, Daddy, Savior, protector in the time of trouble, make all of my battles easier when I'm obedient. You will never let the Devil or his minions hurt me.

There's healing here and around me! There is jubilation, abundant love, blessings, peace, and riches from You, Father. Thank You. I am praying and believe what You say about me, not what the Enemy says. He is a liar and is trying to make me abort the things You have in store for me. I am beautiful and powerful above measure because greater is He that is within me. I now tap into that power You have given me and know I have the victory over any situation.

Father, without You, where would I be? I stretch my hands out to You with exceeding joy and praise. I thank You, Lord, for this walk, journey, peace, joy, happiness, and unconditional love. Death always to my flesh! I know who holds my life in His hands.

Only Your grace and mercy keep me from pulling all my hair out, so I praise You God!

No weapon formed against me shall prosper, and I will always have the victory. No longer am I a victim. I am the head of it all and never the tail because You are with me. Jesus paid the ultimate price for my soul.

Father, You are the Light of the world and so am I. I will let Your light shine through me so that others may see Your good works and give You all the glory (Matthew 5:14, 16, ESV). Everything I do will be in Your name. I give You praises and glory.

Satan, you are forever removed and defeated from my life.

My peace is in keeping my mind stayed on You, God, because You've got me!

I love You, Father. I glorify Your name. Your perfect will shall be done right now. In the name of Jesus. Amen.

REFERENCES

Dictionary.com, *s.v.*, "decree," accessed August 11, 2020, https://www.diction-ary.com/decree.

Dictionary.com, *s.v.*, "declare," accessed August 11, 2020, https://www.diction-ary.com/declare.

ABOUT THE AUTHOR

Tabetha "Tab" Pittman is first and foremost the daughter of the Most High God, wife, mother, GrandDiva aka Mink Mink to her Grandman, daughter, granddaughter, sister, auntie, cousin, and loyal friend. She has a smile and laughter to illuminate the world.

Even though hurt, pain, and shame tried to take her out, God wanted her yes, her heart, and her focus on His glory. He desired this so that one day, she would tell others how she kept walking through the fire with His daily strength, head held high, and classy.

Because of her obedience and love for God, like any father who knows his child, God knew Tabetha was a warrior who would withstand all the Enemy tried to destroy her with. He knew in spite of all her trials, she would be strong enough to fight the hard battles while wearing a beautiful smile.

Tabetha's deliverance is important to the kingdom of light, and God is completing the good work He started in her (Philippians 1:6, ESV).

She has been chosen for a time like this. She knows her destiny is to do God's will and to be a shining light that draws others to Him. Tabetha has been set free from her mind-blocking prison to share what God has placed on her heart for His edification and the upliftment of His kingdom.

Tabetha is a mighty woman of God, the daughter of God, the sister of Jesus Christ, her Savior and deliverer!

"I am an overcomer! I am a daughter who can call those things that are not, as though they were, knowing that my Father, God will work it out for my good (Romans 4:17-NIV).

I am meek but I'm not weak!"-Yvette Benton

CONTACT TABETHA PITTMAN

Connect with Tabetha on her various social media platforms

Facebook: @touchofabundantblessings

Instagram: touch_abundant_blessings

Email: TouchofAbundantblessings10@gmail.com

www.ingramcontent.com/pod-product-compliance
Lightning Source LLC
LaVergne TN
LVHW021451080426
835509LV00018B/2240